Poetry & Short Stories

A Practice Book

by

Charissa Ong Ty

Poetry & Short Stories - A Practice Book by Penwings Publishing
© 2021 by Penwings Publishing. All rights reserved.

Although every precaution has been taken to verify the accuracy of the information contained herein, the author and publisher assume no responsibility for any errors or omissions. No liability is assumed for damages that may result from the use of information contained within.

Books may be purchased by contacting the publisher and author at:
penwingspublishing@gmail.com
Author: Charissa Ong Ty
Assistant Writer: Siti Aishah
Cover Design: Adrianus Harris
Publisher: Penwings Publishing
Editor: Chuah Yiing Zhi
ISBN: 978-967-14227-6-2
1. General 2. Short Story 3. Poetry 4. Self-Help
First Edition

Printed by:
Percetakan Okid Sdn Bhd
No. 2, Jalan SS 13/3C, Subang Jaya Industrial Estate,
47500, Subang Jaya, Selangor, Malaysia.

Published by: Penwings Publishing
Subang Jaya, Selangor Darul Ehsan, Malaysia.

Reviews of the Practice Book

To a lend voice to a new generation of writers and create hungry spaces for their expressions is the generosity of a truly accomplished artist.
- **Loh Siew Meng,** Head of Student Services at Manipal International University

This book is a great gift for writers who seek to get better in writing and it doesn't just end there. It can also help you market your book and pitch it to publishers in hopes to land a publishing deal.
- **Naadhira Zahari,** Editor

The book encourages and motivates me to write better and smarter. It is perfect for writers that are overwhelmed with the limitless information online and do not know where to get started without feeling intimidated or confused by the different techniques which all ends in feeling stressed and discouraged.
- **Elynn Kok,** Author of Words you'd Whisper

You will find this book like a compilation of a "writer's secrets" poured into beautiful pages. Whatever you want to know is here: the foundations, how to draft, how to write an intro and even down to how to design the cover!
- **Nurul Hakimin,** English Teacher

In my opinion, the real highlight is the guide for preparing the manuscript. This isn't any cheap knowledge you can gain anywhere and the information itself has been told from the perspective of a professional publisher.
- **Adibah Atiqa,** Student, Bachelor of Technology (Environment)

As the local creative writing and publishing scene is ever-evolving, Penwings Publishing which is manned by a fresh, innovative and youthful team seeks to bring light to the many blooming talents of Malaysia. I hope to see more and more quality books from them in the near future.
- **Anita Kumaran,** Secondary School Teacher

Table of Contents

Table of Contents

Poetry

Welcome

Hello fellow aspiring writer,

Congratulations on picking up the very first Penwings Poetry & Short Stories Practice Book! You may call it the Penwings Practice book for short. This book is designed to answer popular writing questions in great detail. If you have questions like:

"How can I write better?"

"I don't have confidence in my writing skills."

"How can I start writing impactful poetry and short stories?"

Hence, this book will be the perfect practice book for you. We hope that this practical writing guide takes you one step closer in achieving your writing goals and dreams. It is an important first step you are taking today and all of us here at Penwings Publishing are cheering you on.

Pens at the ready, let's go!

With love,
The Penwings Team

What inspires you to write?

'Why do I write?' is an important question we should ask ourselves constantly as we evolve as writers. Have you ever asked yourself why did you start writing or why has writing piqued your interest?

Any writer around the block would tell you that their lifelong dream is to witness their books sitting beautifully among other popular paperbacks in major bookstores. Although this might seem like a realistic dream to look forward to, simply seeing your books on those bookshelves might not be a strong enough factor for you to keep going. Having passion for writing is merely not enough. It requires deeper motivations, discipline and stamina if you want to reach the finishing line. We're not scaring you, are we?

There's a reason why completing a novel or a short story is seen as a great accomplishment. Not many can last the race. It is particularly important to understand the driving factor of why you want to write because in order to produce impactful work, you would need to have a clear vision of the person you are writing for. Dig deep and reflect on *'Why do I write?'*.

Dream big even if you're just trying it out for the first time. Be open to its potential of turning into something bigger than yourself.

We have prepared some popular examples for this exercise in case you can't think of any at the moment. You may tick more than one box if they apply to you. There are no right or wrong answers to this.

REFRAMING

What inspires you to write?

☐ I want to share my stories with the world and challenge perspectives.

☐ Writing gives me an opportunity to share with others about life lessons that I have been through.

☐ I want to make my country proud when my book gets adapted into a movie or reaches the international bestselling list.

☐ I just want to write for myself and become a better writer.

☐ Writing helps me to relieve stress and keep me calm.

☐ I want to train myself to write short stories first before embarking on a full-fledged novel.

☐ I just want to learn something new!

☐ Writing is just a hobby of mine.

☐ As Toni Morrision says, *"If there's a book that you want to read, but it hasn't been written yet, then you must write it."*

☐ I want to become a famous published author one day so that I can inspire and help aspiring authors like myself navigate this path.

☐ I write because I want to convey important messages to society.

☐ ____

REFRAMING

What inspires you to write?

It is natural for goals to change as time passes by. Always have a backup goal ready in case you achieve your first goal unexpectedly. It happens. Your goals should grow with you. So, setting a big end goal in your life helps you to stay focused and motivates you to move forward despite unfavorable circumstances, potential procrastinations or excuses you will make. Life is full of ups and downs and it will only get harder if you don't set a goal that is capable of scaring you into action.

Realizing a dream that is bigger than yourself will put you to work even if you don't feel like doing so. Inspiration and feelings are fleeting, but habits and discipline are not. In accompaniment to your audacious goal, have smaller weekly and daily goals too. It makes the big goal feel more possible to achieve. Even moving just a little every day imperfectly is progress.

Starting out as a writer can be challenging. Rejection and doubt of your work from yourself and peers is perfectly normal. Failing and learning are important aspects to success. Even on days when you feel incredibly dejected and are wallowing in a pool of self-doubt and fear, remind yourself that Rome wasn't built in a day, and neither will your writing career. Consistency and positivity is key, so keep your chin up, pick up a pen and keep going! You will notice improvements over time.

REFRAMING

Who do you write for?

Before you begin writing, ask yourself these two questions:

"Who do you see picking up your book or clicking the link to read your short story?"
"How are they telling their friends about it?"

Are they young teenagers who are in love or adults looking for a higher purpose? Are you writing for yourself? Different target segments will take you to very different paths. If your reason is to write stories for your own personal creative exploration, then there are no rules! On the other hand, if you desire to publish your work to the public, there are an array of processes and limitations you should be aware of. Does your target segment use English as a second language? Are there simpler words that you can use to substitute big, bombastic words with?

The one thing that defines the success of a book that is publicly published is having a clear vision of who the author is writing for. If they do not have this vision, the story will be too abstract, confusing and unsuitable for public consumption. Understand your potential readers.

Here are some questions we ask whilst interviewing authors that we might represent under our publishing house. You may also do this exercise even if you are on a private writing journey.

Who do you write for?

1. What is their age range? (eg. 16 to 24, 25 to 35)

____

2. What is their primary language?

____

3. What is their language proficiency? (Eg. Primary, Secondary, University)

____

4. What is their attention span? How long can they stay focused on an article or a 3,000 word short story before clicking away?

____

5. What genre do they like or dislike?

____

6. How liberal are they?

____

7. How do they tell their friends about books they love?

____

Short Stories

Foundational Training

Many think that short stories are easier to write compared to full-length novels. It probably is, if you look at it in terms of length and time spent. However, with different formats come different challenges. Making sure you have proper character development, good pacing and timely peaks and dips in your storyline, all whilst keeping a character count can be challenging too. Writing short stories can be a good starting point if your end goal is to become a published writer. Some readers might prefer short stories too as it takes less commitment!

This book serves as foundational training that provides you with an opportunity to understand why certain texts are good or bad. Just like playing music, writing is a skill that needs to be sharpened regularly to improve. It is an art that needs thorough practice and studying over a long period of time. With a good foundation in the basics of writing, you will be able to accelerate your learning process.

We have divided this book into clear sections where we will develop your themes, characters and finally, a complete short story together. There are also proofreading and editing exercises and techniques that will help you enhance and refine your stories. Let's awaken your inner creative spirit and bring out the writer in you!

What Makes A Short Story Good or Bad?

An average short story is about 10,000 words in length while a full-length novel has a minimum of 50,000 words. Flash short stories can be told in less than five hundred words. In the interest of getting our point across quickly, we will be using a couple of flash short stories in the upcoming exercises in this book. Many short stories that have successfully impacted the great worlds of entertainment, science, politics and fiction. Have you ever wondered what makes a short story good? These are some of the criteria we use for manuscript reviews.

1. Interesting Plots

Short stories are capable of evoking emotions while conveying moral themes to their readers in a short amount of time. Writing a compelling fiction story has to feel very real, while writing a non-fiction book should feel like a story when read. Naturally, your plot should be interesting and unique enough along with an easy flow to follow. Research existing plots in the market and try modifying them for a start.

2. Defined Genre & Themes

Define your genre first. By doing this, your book will be correctly cataloged in bookstores and you would have a clear direction of how your book will finally turn out. Your short story should also have a defined theme or key emotion. Is it romance or fantasy? Do you want the reader to feel emotional, hopeful or happy most of the time? Choose a genre and mood that is suitable for your story. As F. Scott Fitzgerald says, *"Find the key emotion, this may be all you need to find your short story."*

3. Characters

A set of characters with interesting strengths and flaws are crucial. The main character's goal is to help develop the main narrative while the supporting characters' roles are to provide comic relief, increase or decrease the complexity of the storyline and give more depth and realism to the setting and environment of the story. Turn your protagonists into antagonists or vice versa to keep it interesting. Good writers make readers thoroughly invested in their characters even though they're only there for support.

4. Grammar & Spelling

Keep in mind that great stories also follow the rules of grammar. This is important because the public already has a common understanding of how language works. Therefore, in order to reduce their mental burden while reading your work and to convey your ideas effectively, you would need to adhere to those rules. There are a variety of tools online to help you work on your grammar and spelling.

5. Good Pacing & Flow

A great short story needs good structure and flow to avoid the story from being too draggy or too abrupt. Drafting an outline is useful before writing. Many good novels and short stories have breaks of peace and comedy in between fast-paced battles to allow the reader some room to relax. You wouldn't want to stress your readers out too much by taking them through a battle that lasts for 200 pages now, would you?

6. Red Flags

Red flags like swear words, murder, suicide, sex, politics or religion are examples of content that might be banned in certain countries. They may narrow your audience due to its censorship. If you still wish to pursue these topics, address them respectfully and creatively. As authors who have public influence, it is our responsibility to be aware of the implications of our writing.

7. Good Language

Simple yet eloquent language in creative writing is important in being understood by your readers. You wouldn't want them to be confused with your jargon and big words. Here's an example of simplification:

Nope - *"She abhors him with a great magnitude of vehemence."*
Yes - *"She hates him with passion."*

If your work features multiple languages, make sure they are distinct from the primary language and used sparingly. Italicize their speech and translate them creatively in your story. With this method, you are able to use imaginary languages while still making total sense.

"Oh, mon dieu!" he exclaimed. For an atheist, he sure calls on God quite a lot.

"Shrikhal gur bar il-hoelil," instructed the head lady of the village. Without a second to lose, two slaves pulled her hair up into a neat bun and fixed on a pair of unblemished pearl earrings.

—

Remember, short stories are short, so do not waste time and space! Every detail has to bring meaning to your whole story. Even though there are no hard or fast rules in writing, these tips are here to help you understand the basics of producing a manuscript. After understanding the basics, feel free to manipulate and stretch the boundaries of each criterion, very much like how Daniel Keyes has done for his novel *Flowers for Algernon*. In his case, he used both childlike and professor-like grammar levels to illustrate the degradation and enhancements of the character's brain development.

"Before breaking the rules, you have to understand how they work and why they were there in the first place. Only after mastering the rules, will you know how to exploit them to your advantage."

Exercise 1: Proofreading

Before you start writing your short story, the first step is to learn how to spot errors that make short stories bad in order to avoid these mistakes in the future.

Let's try out this proofreading exercise first to see if you can spot the mistakes in this short story. We will be focusing on the technical aspects of writing for now. Try to spot for **spelling, grammar, punctuation and sentence structure errors** for this exercise. Highlight or underline different parts of the text that you find these specific errors. The answers are provided at the end of the short story. Don't worry about getting a perfect score, it's all part of the learning process.

Mira

She steped outside after the rain had finally stopped The wet grass wet her slippers slightly and the cool breeze kissed her cheek as she breathed in the air. Her mothers old house in the countryside is now belongs to her after her sudden death. 'About time', she thought to herself. She had suffer.

Tall abundant trees at the forest ahead of her brick house looks sullen and wears out from the heavy rain, hunch, dripping water drops from their green leaves. They resembeld her mother, she realizes.

She went back to inside the house, drifted to the kitchen and switched on the electric kettle for a pot of tea. She tries to remember what her mother sounded like. Silence. That was all she heard. She opened one of the ceramic canister and found the teabags. Only black. Her mothers favorite. Click.

The hot water is ready. She poured the hot water into a porcelain pot and placed one tea bag inside. The steaming, clear water turned light brown and slowly becoms a deep, dark orange color Like innocence, she thought. Born unsullied but humans become more tainted as they grow. She stirs her pot of tea and dropped a little cubes of sugar to the dark orange sea. The sugar cubes melted, infusing the tea with sweetness.

She never meet her father. She was left to grow up alone with her strict single mother. She does never allowed to dress up or wear bright colours. "You'll attract unnecessary attention," she said. "You don't want anyone to prancing over you, would you." Like a puppet, she is stringed to her mother's orders. One mistake and she would witness her mother breaking down. "I just want you to be happy. Cant you see I dont want you to become me?," she sobbed She had only talked to her male classmate that day. "It was only about homework", she pleaded meekly to her worried mother. It wasn't enough evidence. She felt the disappointment seething from her mother and promised her she'd never do that again. Boys. That was *among the thing she had told her to stay away.*

She knew why do her mother was anxious and wary about men. One of them, her father, left her in ruins. Pregnant at eighteen and unwedded. He told her he'd comeback from the city soon to saving her from the death stares and stabbing words of her family and neighbors. It was not in the nature of her community to be forgiving and lovingly when one has tarnished her family's image. Only a husband, a man could save her from this infinity shame but her man never came back.

"Can you believe that girl, Mira, had a child out of wedlock?"

"Tut, tut, tut what a disappointment. Her parents are such great people. Seems like money clearly cant brought up a decent girl."

Months had go by and the baby's arrival was nigh. She delivered the baby in home to avoid deeper shame at hospital.

After hearing the first cries of her daughter., she know she would have to leave the place for a better life. A man-less life.

Did you notice any other mistakes? Write down your thoughts and opinions and discuss them with your teacher or peers.

Exercise 1: Proofreading Answers

Great job! Now, let's go through the corrections together.

Mira

[Paragraph 1]

She **[1] stepped** outside after the rain had finally **[2] stopped. [3] The dew-drenched grass soaked** her slippers slightly and the cool breeze kissed her dimpled cheeks as she breathed in the air. Her **[4] mother's** old house in the **[5] countryside now belongs** to her after her sudden death. 'About time', she thought to herself. **[6] She had suffered enough.**

[1] Spelling error! It's not steped but stepped.

[2] There's a missing full stop after the word stopped.

[3] Sentence structure error. The writer used 'wet' twice in a sentence making it sound redundant and repetitive.

[4] Missing an apostrophe. Punctuation marks are important in writing.

[5] Grammar error. 'Be' verb 'is' is unnecessary.

[6] Another grammar error spotted! Remember, after using 'be' verb 'has', the verb next to it must be in its past participle form. In this case, the answer is "suffered."

[Paragraph 2]

Tall abundant trees **[7] in** the forest ahead of her brick house **[8] looked** sullen and **[9] worn** out from the heavy rain, **[10] hunched,** dripping water drops from their green leaves. They **[11] resembled** her mother, she **[12] realized.**

[7] Wrong preposition here. It should be 'in the forest'. 'In' refers to a place within a large or spacious area while 'at' refers to a specific point of a place.

[8] Wrong tense. The writer is not using past tense consistently in the story.

[9] Not only is 'wears' wrong because trees are a plural form but it is also wrong because the writer uses present tense again.

[10] Wrong tense.

[11] Another spelling error. The correct spelling is 'resembled'.

[12] Wrong tense. Similar to errors 8 and 10.

[Paragraph 3]

She went **[13] back inside** the house, drifted to the kitchen and switched on the electric kettle for a pot of tea. She **[14] tried** to remember what her mother sounded like. Silence. That was all she heard. She opened one of the ceramic **[15] canisters** and found the teabags. Only black. Her **[16] mother's** favorite. Click.

[13] Misuse of the preposition. 'To' is not needed.

[14] Wrong tense.

[15] Grammar error. "Canisters" is the correct word. You're singling that one canister of the many.

[16] Missing an apostrophe.

[Paragraph 4]

The hot water **[17] was** ready. She poured the hot water into a porcelain pot and placed one teabag inside. The steaming, clear water turned light brown and slowly **[18] became** a deep, dark orange **[19] color. Like** innocence, she thought. Born unsullied but humans become more tainted as they grow. She **[20] stirred** her pot of tea and dropped a **[21] few** cubes of sugar **[22] into** the dark orange sea. The sugar cubes melted, infusing the tea with sweetness.

[17] Wrong tense again. It should be written in the past tense.

[18] Tense error.

[19] Missing a full stop after the word 'color." For the books we publish, we usually use American English instead of British English in our texts.

[20] 'Stirred' is the correct tense.

[21] Grammar error. "Little" is used as a quantifier for uncountable nouns. Since 'cubes of sugar' is countable 'few' is the correct quantifier.

[22] Another grammar error! The preposition 'to' refers to a direction of a place or point but 'into' indicates placing something physically inside of something else.

[Paragraph 5]

She never **[23] met** her father. She was left to grow up alone with her strict single mother. She **[24] was** never allowed to dress up or wear bright colors. "You'll attract unnecessary attention," she said. "You don't want anyone **[25] prancing** over you, would **[26] you?**" Like a puppet, she **[27] was [28] strung** to her mother's orders. One mistake and she would witness her mother breaking down. "I just want you to be happy. **[29] Can't** you see I **[30] don't** want you to become me?" she **[31] sobbed. She** had only talked to her male classmate that day. "It was only about homework", she pleaded meekly to her worried mother. It wasn't enough evidence. She felt the disappointment seething from her mother and promised her that she'd never do that again. Boys. That was among the**[32] things** she had told her to **[33] stay away from.**

[23] Wrong tense.

[24] Incorrect verb. 'Does' is redundant, so it should be 'was.'

[25] There are two answers! If you answered 'to prance' or 'prancing' then they are both correct. If your answer is the former, then you should know that after the use of 'to', the verb has to be a root verb.

[26] A question mark is missing after 'you'. The character's mother was asking her a question.

[27] Wrong tense again.

[28] Incorrect past tense of the verb 'string.'

[29] Missing an apostrophe.

[30] Again, the writer missed an apostrophe. Punctuation is crucial when it comes to writing good short stories.

[31] Missing a full stop here after the word 'sobbed.'

[32] Grammar error. 'Among' is used when describing things or people as a group. Hence, 'thing' has to be in plural form, 'things.'

[33] Sentence structure error. Preposition 'from' is needed here to complete the context of the sentence.

[Paragraph 6]

She knew **[34] why her** mother was anxious and wary about men. One of them, her father, left her in ruins. Pregnant at eighteen and unwedded. He told her he'd come back from the city soon to **[35] save** her from the death stares and stabbing words **[36] from** her family and neighbors. It was not in the nature of her community to be forgiving and **[37] loving** when one **[38] had** tarnished her family's image. Only a husband, a man could save her from this **[39] infinite** shame but her man never came back.

[34] 'Do' is unnecessary here.

[35] Of course, after the preposition 'to', the verb must be in its original form.

[36] 'From' is more suitable as a preposition here, indicating she is receiving the terrible things from people around her.

[37] 'Lovingly' is an adverb and in this sentence, an adjective is the correct word to describe her community.

[38] Another wrong use of tense. It must be in the past tense as this all happened in the past.

[39] 'Infinity' is a noun and an adjective, 'infinite' is more suitable here because it describes the immense shame faced by the girl.

[Paragraph 7]

"Can you believe that girl, Mira, had a child out of wedlock?"

"Tut, tut, tut, what a disappointment. Her parents are such great people. Seems like money clearly **[40] can't [41] bring** up a decent girl.

[40] An apostrophe is missing here.

[41] Similar to the preposition 'to', the verb after using the word 'can' must be a root word.

[Paragraph 8]

Months had **[42] gone** by and the baby's arrival was nigh. She delivered the baby **[43] at** home to avoid deeper shame **[44] at the hospital.** After hearing the first cries of her daughter, she **[45] knew** she would have to leave the place for a better life. A man-less life.

[42] Grammar mistake here. After 'had', you must use the past participle of a verb.

[43] 'At' is the correct preposition because it indicates a specific place. 'At home' can also mean, 'in her home'.

[44] Missing the word 'the' to complete the sentence structure.

[45] Wrong tense here. Always remember to keep your tenses consistent.

How many mistakes did you spot? Score yourself:

__/45

Exercise 2: Proofreading & Explanations

Alright, now that you have got a good grasp on the technical aspects to produce a polished manuscript, let's have a look at the other important aspects: **storytelling, character development and pacing.** This is an example of a bad short story but with all technical aspects addressed:

Sarah's Life

Sarah woke up in excitement that morning and got dressed as soon as she had her shower. She was finally going out with Brad. She did her eyebrows and drew eyeliner on her eyes. She wore her favorite black top with her beige pants. Brad called and they went out together. Later, they went for a stroll at the park.

One day, Sarah found her mother lying unconscious on the floor. She quickly called for an ambulance and went to the hospital to see her mother. She couldn't stop feeling worried and waited patiently outside for the results. But, she was glad to know it was nothing serious.

Sarah and Brad's relationship started to blossom but the situation with her mother negatively affected her happiness. Brad didn't understand what she was feeling or how difficult her situation was. He wants to spend more time with her but her mother wouldn't allow it.

Sarah finally ended things with Brad. She wanted peace but couldn't find it at home either. She wanted everything to stop and return to how it was. She sat alone and cried.

A miracle happened. Brad understood and her mother got better. Sarah felt so happy and she agreed to marry Brad. Her mother was also happy and cried tears of joy. The end.

[Paragraph 1]

Sarah woke up in excitement that morning and got dressed as soon as she had her shower. She was finally going out with Brad. She did her eyebrows and drew eyeliner on her eyes. She wore her favorite black top with her beige pants. Brad called and they went out together. Later, they went for a stroll at the park.

Explanation: The beginning of the story is too abrupt. The main characters (Sarah and Brad) have little to no introduction and there was no clear description of their relationship. This introduction also lacked vivid images of the setting, premise and location of where the characters were or how their date went. Emotions are also lacking in this paragraph.

Try rewriting this introduction:

____

____

____

____

____

____

____

____

____

____

____

____

____

[Paragraph 2]

One day, Sarah found her mother lying unconscious on the floor. She quickly called for an ambulance and went to the hospital to see her mother. She couldn't stop feeling worried and waited patiently outside for the results. But, she was glad to know it was nothing serious.

Explanation: Story pacing is the issue here. The story jumps too quickly into the mother's sickness and there is no smooth transition from Sarah's date to finding her unconscious mother.

[Paragraph 3]

Sarah and Brad's relationship started to blossom but the situation with her mother negatively affected her happiness. Brad didn't understand what she was feeling or how difficult her situation was. He wants to spend more time with her but her mother wouldn't allow it.

Explanation: Detail and relationship building is the issue here. The lack of development between Sarah and Brad leaves readers hanging about how their relationship actually blossomed. There is also no explanation about the characters' personalities which makes the whole story feel quite transactional.

[Paragraph 4]

Sarah finally ended things with Brad. She wanted peace but couldn't find it at home either. She wanted everything to stop and return to how it was. She sat alone and cried.

Explanation: The ambiance of her home as a setting is not present, resulting in confusing imagery and flow. As a reader, you won't know where she is crying, and how she ended it with Brad. As a writer, describing her environment and articulating thoughts can help create a more complex main character.

[Paragraph 5]

A miracle happened. Brad understood and her mother got better. Sarah felt so happy and she agreed to marry Brad. Her mother was also happy and cried tears of joy. The end.

Explanation: The ending is too abrupt and has zero connection with the rest of the story. Overall, this short story lacks finesse because it's missing creativity, an important theme, a setting, and character development.

Try rewriting this story in your notebook.

Getting Started

Now that you have a higher sensitivity for both technical and basic storytelling mistakes, it is time for us to dive deeper into all of the criteria mentioned in the previous chapter.

Before you get straight into writing a full short story, you will need to think of a genre, theme, setting and characters. We'll go through these steps together one by one.

A well-paced narrative with a well-defined theme, setting and character development plan will set the track for a great short story!

"If you can quit, do. There are other easier ways to make a living. But if you can't, if the stories have to be told and the characters in your head won't shut up, then never give up."
- unknown

Exercise 3: Defining your Genre & Theme

Choosing Your Genre

When you go to a bookstore, do you find yourself gravitating to a specific genre shelf? Humans live to categorize. We do so to optimize how we process information. Needless to say, without a genre, your readers would not know how to advocate your work. A short story without a genre is like a broken compass that brings your narrative nowhere.

You can pick one or two genres that will define your short story. Most stories have more than one genre. This includes the Harry Potter series which is categorized as both fantasy and young adult fiction. What will your genre be? Will it be chick-lit or dystopian? Romance or horror? Think of it this way. If you were to look for your book on Amazon, where would your book be categorized? Refer to those categories. We'll wait.

Done? It might be a little overwhelming at first, but it certainly helps you in the long run when you need to market and sell your book. Try looking for similar books to yours on those platforms and identify which genres they fall into.

Write it down below. Don't stress yourself out too much, it's bound to change as you progress further.

Main Genre:

____

Supporting Genre:

____

Defining Your Theme

All great stories have noticeable themes. It is one of the main ingredients of writing that gives your story a sense of purpose. Whether you're writing romance, fantasy, horror, or comedy, your theme is pivotal in introducing depth in your narrative. Think of messages you want to portray in your short story and develop it creatively with your characters and setting. It is the reader's task to extract your messages from your story be it consciously or subconsciously. To illustrate the differences between Genres and Themes, here's an example applied to 'Frozen' by Disney.

Story: Frozen by Disney
Genre: Adventure, Fantasy
Theme: Family, friendship, self-identity, romantic love

To help you get started, we have researched six different examples of common themes that are prevalent in the market.

1. Romantic Love

Everyone loves a good love story whether it is about unrequited love or one that ends happily. 'The Notebook' by Nicholas Sparks is a prime example of a love tale that brings readers to tears.

2. Coming of Age

Also known as bildungsroman, this theme surrounds the development of the main character from losing their innocence to discovering the journey to adulthood. 'Little Women' by Louisa May Alcott employs the coming-of-age theme where the female characters go through trials and tribulations of growing up.

3. Good vs. Evil

The story of good fighting evil will always draw the attention of readers. The classic battle between J.K. Rowling's Harry Potter and Voldemort has kept her fans engaged with the series for more than two decades.

4. Family Love

If you have read M. L. Stedman's 'The Light Between The Oceans' or Mitch Albom's 'For One More Day', then you would know the emotions and feelings evoked when you read a touching story on family relationships.

5. Friendship

Harry, Ron and Hermoine's friendship is a great example that will always have a special place in the hearts of Potterheads. Their friendship is portrayed beautifully throughout the series.

6. Revenge

As Homer says in 'The Iliad', *"Revenge is far sweeter than flowing honey."* Revenge is a common theme in many stories where a conflict is present and a character strives to seek revenge over his or her enemy while exploring the moral consequences of vengeance. Readers find joy living vicariously through these characters.

It is of utmost importance that you write about something you're passionate about. To quote Maya Angelou, *There is no greater agony than bearing an untold story inside you.* Let's see what ideas you have in your brilliant mind by jotting down the themes of your choice! Don't limit yourself.

Theme 1:

____

Theme 2:

____

Theme 3:

____

Theme 4:

____

Exercise 4: Visualizing Settings

Have you ever read a dystopian or fantasy novel that is set in a world completely different than ours, like Suzanne Collins' 'The Hunger Games'? Or a story that is set in nineteenth-century England, in Jane Austen's 'Pride and Prejudice'? Although these two stories are set in different times and places, the settings portrayed are vivid and described with sensory details and imagery. To put it plainly, a setting defines the **location, time and social environment** of your story.

Readers love visualizing and escaping to the fictitious worlds they're reading about. Therefore, it is your obligation to write a clear setting in your narrative. Most importantly, a good setting establishes the context and mood of your story. Defining a setting beforehand gives you a chance to dive deep and wide into your imaginary worlds. We have the absolute power of designing the home where all our imaginary friends live. Make it as real as possible by adding in unique details.

You may add extra environments and sub-timelines (for you sci-fi buffs) after defining the main setting and timeline. Here's a setting example for a short story.

Location:
Yau Ma Tei, Hong Kong

Timeline:
Modern day, Present, Year 2021

External Environment:
(Main City) Gloomy, Bustling, High density, Grey, Cramped

Internal Environment:
(Home) Warm, Cosy, Quiet, Small, Tranquil, Beige

People:
Always in a rush, Stoic, Middle class

—

And here's an example of a **setting being applied** in a short story:

Faith tries to catch her breath as she carelessly makes her way through the bustling crowd. It's a quarter to six and Nathan Road is packed as usual. She passes by Yau Ma Tei station and notices the long line of people queuing to go down the escalator, to the trains. What's more, the drizzling rain motivated a larger crowd of people to get back home as early as possible. She would probably wait for a little while until the crowd thins out. No way is she going to be caught in the middle of a bunch of pushy, sweaty, damp white collars again. The only reason for her leaving the comfort of her cozy couch is to satiate her craving for bubble tea.

It has been a while since she last drank one, but today, she decided that neither rain nor storm could stop her from getting that thirty-dollar cup of sweet brown sugar milk tea with chewy boba. She takes a sharp right from the station and walks straight ahead until the bright yellow lights of the bubble tea shop sign are in full view. Filled with joy, she enters the shop and lets the smell of frothy milk and caramelized sugar waft through her little button nose. She frowns, only to realize that the drink she wanted to order was no longer in stock.

Example of the short story with **no setting applied:**

Faith tries to catch her breath as she makes her way through the crowd. As she keeps walking, she notices the long line of people queuing to go down the escalator to the trains. She would probably wait for a little while until the crowd thins out on the way back. The only reason for her going out *is to satiate her craving for bubble tea. It has been a while since she last drank one, but today, she decided that neither rain nor storm could stop her from getting it. Filled with joy, she enters the shop. She frowns, only to realize that the drink she wanted to order was no longer in stock.*

—

As you can see here, the lack of setting description makes it difficult for your readers to understand where the character is, how the bubble tea shop looks like, or where the people are queuing at. Try creating a descriptive setting in your short story so your readers are able to fully experience your writing. Time to get cracking on your setting!

Now, you have a go. We've added extra fields for you if you need them.

Location:

____

Timeline:

____

External Environment 1:

____

External Environment 2:

____

Internal Environment 1:

____

People in External Environments:

____

People in Internal Environments:

____

Exercise 5: Creating Your Characters

The best stories in the market are not just about interesting plots, but they also revolve around iconic characters. Your characters are just as crucial as your storyline. Some might argue that your character's personality, flaws, and development are the backbone of a good storyline. Ernest Hemmingway says, *"When writing a novel, a writer should create living people; people, not characters. A character is a caricature."*

So, creating characters with whom readers can relate to as a human, level up the compelling factor of your story. Don't be afraid to give your characters quirks, flaws, pet peeves, disorders or mental illnesses. The bigger the flaw, the bigger the challenge they have to face and the more creative your character has to be to overcome them. It definitely makes it more inspiring and interesting when readers read them. Doesn't it make you think about how and why humans are created? We are all main characters with flaws and it's up to us on how we write our story and rise above them. In this exercise, we have organized a few steps that can help you create your main characters.

Step 1: Appearance.

What does your main character look like? Describe your main character's appearance and the little details like tattoos and scars if they are critical for story progression. Describing your characters in too much detail also restricts your reader's imagination on how they want the main character to look like. Remember, your reader is your co-writer. Letting your reader know the character's age, gender identity and body build is the bare minimum. Not letting your readers know this basic information will infuriate them. It's difficult to connect with a character when the reader can't visualize them.

Main Character's Description (Lottie):

a) Tall and lanky
b) Thin
c) Frizzy red hair with split ends
d) Fair-skinned
e) High school girl

Example: *Despite the bustling crowd in the hallway, Lottie's tall figure and fiery red hair stood out. Just before school, she attempted taming her wild head of hair with a straightening iron, but it was to no avail. She gave up after her fifth try. She sighed in defeat and accepted that it will serve as a homing beacon to every disciplinary teacher in school, again.*

Step 2: Personality.

What are your character's strengths and weaknesses? Create a three-dimensional character with depth, motivations, flaws and personality traits.

Main Character's Personality (Lottie):

a) Cheerful
b) Bubbly
c) Studious
d) Friendly

Example: *To the outside world, Lottie is a cheerful and bubbly person. She scores good grades, enough for her to be recognized in school as the average student. Not quite a dork, but not quite popular either.*

Step 3: Relationship with other characters.

To develop a realistic environment around your character, they should have unique relationships with other characters. This will give the reader a sense of how the character acts around different characters by giving the readers access to the main character's thoughts and actions.

Main Character's Bond with Other Characters (Lottie):

a) Has a great relationship with her friends and teachers
b) Finds it hard to compete with her two sisters' success

Example: *Lottie has many good friends and is friendly with everyone, including her teachers at school. Little do they know that she is struggling for approval at home. Her two sisters were always outshining her in every aspect and she finds it hard to please her parents.*

Step 4: Relationship with their environments.

Adding this layer to your character is also a good way to create a well-rounded and realistic character. It displays what your character advocates.

Main Character's Bond with The Environment:

a) Used to be wealthy but now lives modestly
b) Adapted to lifestyle changes

Example: *Lottie's family used to be quite well-off. They lived in a large house with sixteen rooms although it was just her father, mother and herself. But, ever since her parents got divorced, she has since moved into a smaller home with her father, step-mother and two ridiculously overachieving step-sisters.*

Step 5: Dreams.

Define their dreams and aspirations. This is significant as it would potentially drive your entire plot.

Main Character's Dream (Lottie):

a) To move to New York City and live her dreams
b) To be independent from her family

Example: *Lottie always dreamed of leaving her old town and moving to New York City. "The city seen from the Queensboro Bridge is always the city seen for the first time, in its first wild promise of all the mystery and the beauty of the world." That is one of her favorite quotes from The Great Gatsby and it is this quote that sparked her dream to leave her stuffy, little house.*

—

After understanding these steps, are you ready to create your own characters? Give it a try!

Main Character's Name:

____

Appearance:

____

Personality:

____

Relationships with other characters:

____

____

Relationships with the environment:

____

____

____

Dreams:

____

____

Great job! You may repeat this exercise for your supporting characters as well.

Time to Hustle!

In this chapter, you will begin building the structure of your own short story! After understanding the foundations of a short story from choosing a genre to creating your characters, you are ready to outline the events of your story. Many writers tend to *follow their heart* and *see where it goes* when they write. While it seems like a perfectly reasonable thing to do, you may jump from idea to idea without settling and that might increase the risk of not completing your story. An outline will provide you with a tangible guide that could help organize your ideas into your story better.

Always keep in mind that short stories are called 'short' for a reason and dragging a short story will induce feelings of boredom. You may apply these principles when you are ready to write a full-length novel. But for this practice, let's write a short story with at least 3,000 words.

As the best-selling author, Neil Gaiman says, *"Short stories are tiny windows into other worlds and other minds and other dreams. They're journeys you can make to the far side of the universe and still be back in time for dinner."*

Exercise 6: Drafting an Outline

We will now move on to drafting a high-level outline of your short story! Writing an outline will help construct a high-level linear storyline so that your theme is able to present itself well in your plot. To help you get started, we have made a template outline for your convenience. Try it out on the next page!

Every iconic story has a main storyline. Complexities and side stories are usually added in later. We shall use an outline template by Victoria Naughton called 'Picture it'. It uses the acronym S.T.O.R.Y. Here's an example of it being applied to J.K. Rowling's Harry Potter & the Philosopher's Stone.

Title: Harry Potter & The Philosopher's Stone	By: J.K. Rowling	Version # 1
S	**Setting:** 1990's England town & Alnwick's Castle at Hogwarts	
T	**Talking Characters:** A young boy who survived an evil sorcerer. Two best friends & teachers at Hogwarts.	
O	**Oops, Problem:** A piece of treasure in school is in danger of being stolen by an evil sorcerer.	
R	**Attempts to resolve:** The young boy and his two best friends rush to stop the evil sorcerer.	
Y	**Yes, resolved! :** The stone is destroyed and the boy is rescued by the headmaster.	

Now, you try it. We have put in an extra column for versioning because you might have multiple variations of the main storyline. Copy this template into another exercise book if you need more. It would be easier to compare them all if you need feedback from your peers or teachers.

Title:	By:	Version #
S	Setting:	
T	Talking Characters:	
O	Oops Problem:	
R	Attempts to resolve:	
Y	Yes, resolved! :	

Exercise 7: Writing your introduction

Great job! After you've squeezed all of your great ideas into a high-level outline, your introduction is ready to be written. This is known to be the hardest part of the writing process, but not to worry, we're here with you.

You can jump into the main event of your plot for a moment to get the readers excited, then flash them back to an earlier timeline where it all began. You may also start off with a calm introduction to your characters and environments from a third-person point of view with a simple monologue. Either way works, you just have to get creative with it. You're the director of your very own movie!

Your theme will slowly emerge as your readers start to read the story. Your introduction does not need to be perfect the first time. Write the best as you could on your first try and proceed with the rest of the story. Edit your introduction with a fresh pair of eyes and mindset the next day.

Here's a tip to help you overcome that feeling of discontent with your writing and the urge to just focus on a specific portion. Set a time limit of 15 minutes to write your introduction. Once the time is up, move on with the rest of your story. It can be tough to set a time limit but take this as a challenge to take your skills to the next level. Let's begin!

Exercise 7: Write your introduction

Exercise 7: Write your introduction

Exercise 7: Write your introduction

Exercise 7: Write your introduction

Exercise 7: Write your introduction

Exercise 8: 100 Words-a-Day Challenge

As they always say, practice makes perfect! Consistently writing is a great way to improve your skill. Write 100 words of your story every day before you go to bed. Set a realistic time for yourself and commit to it. This way, you would be able to maintain your flow on paper. Do not stress over one paragraph over and over again. Just keep writing. Our goal here is to form a healthy writing habit! Discipline is crucial as it does not depend on the inconsistency of feelings to produce continuous output.

There are also writers who 'get into the zone' and end up completing 2000 words in a sitting. In the end, it depends on which process works best for you. Just don't stop writing. Timebox yourself if you have to but always try to maintain a consistent discipline of writing.

You can edit your short story after you have completed it from end to end. Kazuo Ishiguro wrote his Nobel Prize Winner for Literature, '*The Remains of the Day*' in just four weeks but that doesn't mean his manuscript didn't go through numerous stages of editing and proofreading after that! We'll go through more editing and proofreading exercises until you are pleased with the final outcome. Alright, let's begin!

Exercise 8: 100 Words-a-Day Challenge

Exercise 8: 100 Words-a-Day Challenge

Exercise 8: 100 Words-a-Day Challenge

Exercise 8: 100 Words-a-Day Challenge

Exercise 8: 100 Words-a-Day Challenge

Exercise 8: 100 Words-a-Day Challenge

Exercise 8: 100 Words-a-Day Challenge

Exercise 8: 100 Words-a-Day Challenge

Exercise 8: 100 Words-a-Day Challenge

Exercise 8: 100 Words-a-Day Challenge

Exercise 8: 100 Words-a-Day Challenge

Exercise 8: 100 Words-a-Day Challenge

Exercise 8: 100 Words-a-Day Challenge

Exercise 8: 100 Words-a-Day Challenge

Exercise 8: 100 Words-a-Day Challenge

Exercise 8: 100 Words-a-Day Challenge

Exercise 8: 100 Words-a-Day Challenge

Exercise 8: 100 Words-a-Day Challenge

Exercise 8: 100 Words-a-Day Challenge

Exercise 8: 100 Words-a-Day Challenge

Exercise 8: 100 Words-a-Day Challenge

Exercise 8: 100 Words-a-Day Challenge

Exercise 8: 100 Words-a-Day Challenge

Exercise 8: 100 Words-a-Day Challenge

Exercise 8: 100 Words-a-Day Challenge

Exercise 8: 100 Words-a-Day Challenge

Exercise 8: 100 Words-a-Day Challenge

Exercise 8: 100 Words-a-Day Challenge

Exercise 8: 100 Words-a-Day Challenge

Exercise 8: 100 Words-a-Day Challenge

Exercise 8: 100 Words-a-Day Challenge

Exercise 8: 100 Words-a-Day Challenge

Exercise 8: 100 Words-a-Day Challenge

Exercise 8: 100 Words-a-Day Challenge

Exercise 8: 100 Words-a-Day Challenge

Exercise 8: 100 Words-a-Day Challenge

Exercise 8: 100 Words-a-Day Challenge

Exercise 8: 100 Words-a-Day Challenge

Exercise 8: 100 Words-a-Day Challenge

Exercise 8: 100 Words-a-Day Challenge

Exercise 9: Proofreading your work

Proofreading and editing are the most tedious but important steps in writing. Check your grammar and read your story again and again with a pair of fresh eyes. Edit sections of your story that you feel needs more work. Get rid of irrelevant parts that do not add to the plot. Ask yourself, if this character didn't exist, can my story still be told? Do not clutter your story with unnecessary characters and problems that only confuse the reader. Highlight errors based on criteria like grammar, red flags, or sentences that could be improved on, just like the exercise we did earlier in the book!

Self-awareness and self-editing is a trained skill that will only improve through a lot of practice. Rewrite your story again after you have gone over your first edit.

Exercise 9: Proofread & Edit

Exercise 9: Proofread & Edit

Exercise 9: Proofread & Edit

Exercise 9: Proofread & Edit

Exercise 9: Proofread & Edit

Exercise 9: Proofread & Edit

Exercise 9: Proofread & Edit

Exercise 9: Proofread & Edit

Exercise 9: Proofread & Edit

Exercise 9: Proofread & Edit

Exercise 9: Proofread & Edit

Exercise 9: Proofread & Edit

Exercise 9: Proofread & Edit

Exercise 9: Proofread & Edit

Exercise 9: Proofread & Edit

Exercise 9: Proofread & Edit

Exercise 9: Proofread & Edit

Exercise 9: Proofread & Edit

Exercise 9: Proofread & Edit

Exercise 9: Proofread & Edit

Exercise 9: Proofread & Edit

Exercise 9: Proofread & Edit

Exercise 9: Proofread & Edit

Exercise 9: Proofread & Edit

Exercise 9: Proofread & Edit

Exercise 9: Proofread & Edit

Exercise 9: Proofread & Edit

Exercise 9: Proofread & Edit

Exercise 9: Proofread & Edit

Exercise 9: Proofread & Edit

Exercise 9: Proofread & Edit

Exercise 9: Proofread & Edit

Exercise 9: Proofread & Edit

Exercise 9: Proofread & Edit

Exercise 9: Proofread & Edit

Exercise 9: Proofread & Edit

Exercise 9: Proofread & Edit

Exercise 9: Proofread & Edit

Exercise 9: Proofread & Edit

Exercise 9: Proofread & Edit

Exercise 9: Proofread & Edit

Exercise 9: Proofread & Edit

Preparing for Manuscript Submissions

In this chapter, we will go through the basic steps of submitting your manuscript to a publisher or an agent! It might sound simple but in reality, many aspiring writers out there lack basic knowledge of sending emails to publishers.

When sending in your manuscript, make sure that your compilation of short stories is typed in a Microsoft Word document or converted into a PDF format. Sending a whole manuscript typed in the body of an email is a big no-no. It is difficult for documentation and reference among proofreaders in the company. Alternatively, if you wish to send a few chapters only, make sure that you include a detailed summary of your whole manuscript. This will be very helpful as the publisher will be able to grasp the theme and concept of the manuscript. They need this to perform potential market analysis. Publishers get hundreds of submissions weekly, therefore it would be ideal to keep your submission articulate, polite and opportunistic.

Last but certainly not least, please remember to introduce yourself. First impressions are everything. Therefore, you would want to make yourself interesting and pleasant to work with.

These practices will come in handy if you are thinking of writing a full 300-page novel!

Exercise 10: Submission Form

In this exercise, we will practice submitting your completed manuscript to a publisher.

This form helps you:

a) Analyze your competitor's standing against your own and empower you to think in a bigger picture.

b) To enable the publisher to understand your book and you better! Write an eye-catching preview of your story so that the publisher will take notice.

c) To give the publisher a good idea on how to market your book and story to a potential audience.

Exercise 10: Submission Form

Title of book:

____

____

No. of pages:

____

Genre:

____

____

Themes:

____

____

Description/Summary:

____

____

Exercise 10: Submission Form

Books like mine that are in the market now:

Exercise 10: Submission Form

How is my title unique or better than other books on the market?

____

____

____

____

____

When and why did I write this book?

____

____

____

____

Exercise 10: Submission Form

Is this title currently published anywhere else? (eg. as an ebook, online, internationally, locally) Please state.

———————————————————————————

———————————————————————————

———————————————————————————

———————————————————————————

Designing a beautiful cover

People say to never judge a book by its cover. But let's not kid ourselves, because who wouldn't want to own aesthetically pleasing books? A beautifully designed book cover will attract readers at first glance and have them pick up your book out of hundreds. First impressions are everything.

If you are a book hoarder like us, a beautiful book cover is a great deciding factor if we end up taking it home with us or not. Essentially, beautiful covers are quite important in this highly saturated book market. While that is not the case all the time, iconic covers boost your chances of being on the best-selling list because readers will be more familiar with your brand, especially if you have more than one book. Below are some of the steps that you could do to design your own book cover!

Step 1

Sketch your idea on a piece of paper. Don't worry if you can't draw, google references online and get a rough sketch going because it will help you with step 2.

Step 2

Find an illustrator. If you think you don't have the skills or time to do digital art, hiring an illustrator to help you is highly recommended. There are many platforms you can search for amazing, affordable illustrators like Instagram, Fiverr and Behance. These platforms are great to connect with creatives from all over the world. To search for artists on social network platforms, these are some hashtags that you might find useful: #illustration #digitalillustration #digitalart #artwork #graphicdesigner

Step 3

Understand the mood of your book. Pick a theme that suits the genre of your stories and create a mood board to have a better visual of how you want your cover to look. It is also important to communicate with your illustrators and ask them if they are capable of producing illustrations based on your references and theme. Here is an example of a mood board:

Image Credits (all images are from *unsplash.com*)

Keep in mind if you are planning on a trilogy or a sequel to your book. Your book cover should have a strong, unique visual brand while being modular enough for it to be modified slightly. Stephanie Meyer's *Twilight* series illustrates a strong visual brand.

She uses:

a. Consistent color scheme of red, white and black on her covers.
b. Consistent font for titles and layout.
c. Clear elements that are clean and easily identifiable from afar.

Image Credit: *stepheniemeyer.com*

Step 4

Get an ISBN barcode if you're thinking of selling your books on any major online or offline platform. ISBN stands for International Standard Book Number and consists of 13 digits. It acts as a product identifier used by publishers, retail bookstores, libraries and other supply chain participants for ordering, listing, stock control and sales records purposes. It is also easier for booksellers, distributors, or wholesalers to promote and sell your book. You generally need a new ISBN for each new edition of your work. Thus, a hardcover edition of a book would carry a different ISBN than a paperback. If your book is edited 30% and more, it would be defined as a new edition.

For Malaysians, you may apply for an ISBN code in accordance to the criteria set by Perpustakaan Negara. The ISBN code may be provided to you in numbers only, therefore you would need to type in the barcode number into any online barcode generator to generate a pdf version of the barcode. Your designer should then be able to open it up in a vector format and place it at the back of your book easily. One code is unique to one title and edition of a book.

Get more information about ISBN codes on isbn-international.org.

Step 5

Your cover should include a title and your name. Other than the beautiful cover, extra elements like 'rewards badges' from competitions can boost your sales! To get these 'reward badges' all you have to do is pre-submit your work to relevant competitions before the launch.

If you've received an award after launching, simply edit the cover and place the badge over it for your next reprint, or print the stickers separately and have your distributors stick them on all the books currently displayed in bookstores. It's also encouraged to add short quote recommendations from readers, book reviewers, or other book authors! Great reviews sell books.

Exercise 11: Crafting A Cover Letter

It may seem trivial, but your cover letter is the first thing your publisher will read. It is their first impression of your writing. Publishers have thousands of manuscripts and e-mails to go through resulting in high rejection rates. In this exercise, pour in the same amount of passion in your cover letter as in your manuscript! Here is an example of a bad cover letter. You wouldn't want to write it like this:

"hi,

I am writing this letter for you to publish my manuscript. So, how much profit margin would I get? Do i need to pay anything? Should i attach my manuscript here? Do u want the full one or just the first chapter?

Tony"

This cover letter is **bad** because it:

a) Is demanding
b) Asks for profit margins immediately
c) Focuses on making money
d) Has no attachments
e) Has no proper introduction
f) Has spelling and grammatical errors in the email

Here are some tips on crafting a **good** cover letter:

a) Write an introduction. Briefly introduce yourself.
b) Attach your full manuscript.
c) State the genre of the manuscript, the target audience and books that are similar to your story.
d) Mention your synopsis and what is unique about your story.

e) Acknowledge the publisher's genre of choice and books they publish
   (shows that you have done your research)

This is an example of a **good** cover letter:
(Side note: *Demian* by Hermann Hesse is a real book and it's so good!)

"Dear Sir/Madam,

My name is Hermann Hesse and I am a writer who wishes to have my title represented by your publishing company. George Publishing has been my primary choice from the get-go as I truly admire the quality of novels, marketing efforts and unique themes your company represents.

I acknowledge that one of your preferred book genres is bildungsromans or stories about self-growth. My book touches on the theme of self-actualization but with a touch of magical realism. My book is similar to Salinger's 'The Catcher of the Rye' theme of losing innocence. Attached in this email is my full manuscript of 'Demian.'

The story follows young Emil Sinclair, the protagonist of the novel who struggles to find his true identity as a result of growing up in a seemingly religious household while being exposed to the cruelty of the real world. He is conflicted because he feels that he isn't like his holy family but at the same time he could not bring himself to do horrible things like his schoolmates. He is confused with himself and tries to seek help from other figures.

The target audience of this novel are teenagers and adults alike who enjoy the themes of discovering one's identity and self-growth.

Thank you for taking the time to read this. I look forward to hearing from you.

Regards,

Hermann Hesse
01X-XXXXXX

Exercise 11: Crafting A Cover Letter

Now it's time for you to write your own cover letter! Give it a go.

Exercise 11: Crafting A Cover Letter

Poetry

Foundational Training

Do you think you've got what it takes to be the next Keats or Lang Leav? If one of your dreams is to publish a poetry book, it is always great to practice and read consistently. Read like a publisher, not like a reader.

In this section of the practice book, we will be focusing on the world of poetry. There are no definite rules when it comes to writing poetry but there are ways you can spark long-lasting sentiments in your readers with these fundamentals, we have analyzed throughout the years of being in this industry.

What makes a poem good or bad?

Writing poems can be a fun and liberating way to express your emotions healthily and deepen your vocabulary. With the increased use of social media, many aspiring poets have taken up the opportunity to showcase their poetic works online. But, what makes a poem good and captivating? The answer to this question is subjective to every reader. However, let's observe the general consensus as to what makes poetry 'good'.

Good language and story

Good poetry is all about your precision with words and language as well as your ability to tell a story in a concise manner. With the right words, you will be able to express your message and story in a few lines as portrayed in 'Harlem' by Langston Hughes. It is one of Hughes' most notable poems, highlighting the lives of immigrants and their dreams for a better life in America. He used only 11 short lines!

Vivid images

One of the things that makes poetry amazing is the beautiful, poetic metaphors that poets use to help paint vivid images in their readers' minds. It is your job as a poet to paint pictures through words so that your readers are able to visualize them without you needing to be physically present to read to them. Make your readers an accomplice to your story-telling. Using literal words might limit the imagination of your readers so this is where figurative language comes in handy!

Rhythm and meters

These elements give your poetry good flow. Without these tools, your poems are in danger of being draggy, monotonous and awkward.

Exercise 1: Rhyming

In this exercise, we will be focusing on rhymes! Great poetry does not necessarily need to rhyme but rhymes are great if you are going for nostalgia. It is also good practice as it limits your choice of vocabulary by challenging you to use substitute words to convey your message. There are a lot of rhyme schemes you can follow or come up with for this exercise.

Four popular rhyme schemes include:
ABAB,
CDCD,
AABBA,
and AABB.

Below are examples of popular rhyme schemes:

William Shakespeare - "Sonnet 18"

Shall I compare thee to a summer's day?	**A**
Thou art more lovely and more temperate.	**B**
Rough winds do shake the darling buds of May,	**A**
And summer's lease hath all too short to date.	**B**

Robert Frost - "Nothing Gold Can Stay"

Nature's first green is gold,	**A**
Her hardest hue to hold.	**A**
Her early leaf's a flower;	**B**
But only so an hour.	**B**
Then leaf subsides to leaf.	**C**
So Eden sank to grief,	**C**
So dawn goes down to day.	**D**
Nothing gold can stay.	**D**

Different letters signify different sounds. Rhymes help exude a sense of flair to your poetry. However, it is also important to note that you can't just mix random jargon in your poems that sound similar just to rhyme.

Here's a challenge. Good poets always rise to the challenge. Ready to conquer this exercise? Define the type of rhyming scheme that's being used by filling in the dashes on the side with ABAB, ABCB, AABBA or AABB.

Challenge 1:

John Keat - "Bright star, would I were steadfast as thou art"

Bright star, would I were stedfast as thou art—   ____

    Not in lone splendour hung aloft the night   ____

And watching, with eternal lids apart,   ____

    Like nature's patient, sleepless Eremite,   ____

The moving waters at their priestlike task   ____

    Of pure ablution round earth's human shores,   ____

Or gazing on the new soft-fallen mask   ____

    Of snow upon the mountains and the moors—   ____

No—yet still stedfast, still unchangeable,   ____

    Pillow'd upon my fair love's ripening breast,   ____

To feel for ever its soft fall and swell,   ____

    Awake for ever in a sweet unrest,   ____

Still, still to hear her tender-taken breath,   ____

And so live ever—or else swoon to death.   ____

Challenge 2:

William Blake - "The Chimney Sweeper"

A little black thing among the snow,   ____

Crying "weep! 'weep!" in notes of woe!   ____

"Where are thy father and mother? Say?" ___
"They are both gone up to the church to pray. ___

Because I was happy upon the heath, ___
And smil'd among the winter's snow, ___
They clothed me in the clothes of death, ___
And taught me to sing the notes of woe. ___

And because I am happy and dance and sing, ___
They think they have done me no injury, ___
And are gone to praise God and his Priest and King, ___
Who make up a heaven of our misery." ___

Here are the answers!

Challenge 1: ABAB, ABAB, ABAC, AA
Challenge 2: AABB, ABAB, ABAB

Exercise 2: Rhythm & Meters

Rhythm and meters define a balanced flow and tone in your poem. Unless you are writing free verse poems, stressed and unstressed syllables influence the way we read them. When you read a poem out loud, you will tend to hear a pattern; most commonly known as the flow. It gives poetry a sense of music when good rhythm and meters are applied.

Also, maintaining the number of syllables is a way to ensure a good rhythm. Keep the same amount of syllables per line if you can but one or two differences won't be a crime. This is important for you to understand because as a page-poet, you will not be around to read these poems aloud to your readers. They would have to match your expectations when they read it aloud on their own.

Here's an exercise for you to try! Discover the rhythm and meters used in the first stanza of William Wordsworth's 'I Wandered Lonely as a Cloud.' Don't worry, it's easy!

Count the number of syllables and write them on the side of each line. Underline words you find yourself stressing as you read this poem out loud. *Stressing* means that you spend more time on the word, compared to words you just pass by.

I wandered lonely as a cloud, ____

That floats on high o'er vales and hills, ____

When all at once I saw a crowd, ____

A host, of golden daffodils; ____

Beside the lake, beneath the trees, ____

Fluttering and dancing in the breeze. ____

Check your answers! Was it similar to what we had in mind?

"I wandered _lone_ly as a _cloud_,	**8**
That _floats_ on _high_ o'er _vales_ and _hills_,	**9**
When _all_ at _once_ I _saw_ a _crowd_,	**8**
A _host_, of golden daffo_dils_;	**8**
Beside the _lake_, ben_eath_ the _trees_,	**8**
Flutte_ring_ and _dancing_ in the _breeze_."	**9**

The underlined words are the stressed syllables that form a rhythm and a tone to the stanza. As an author, your aim is to close the gap between expected outcome and reality.

Let's try this activity one more time.
Here's the first stanza of John Keat's 'To Autumn'.

Season of mists and mellow fruitfulness,	____
Close bosom-friend of the maturing sun;	____
Conspiring with him how to load and bless	____
With fruit the vines that round the thatch-eves run;	____
To bend with apples the moss'd cottage-trees,	____
And fill all fruit with ripeness to the core;	____
To swell the gourd, and plump the hazel shells	____
With a sweet kernel; to set budding more,	____
And still more, later flowers for the bees,	____
Until they think warm days will never cease,	____
For summer has o'er-brimm'd their clammy cells.	____

How are your answers? Is it similar to ours too?

Season of *mists* and *mellow fruit*fulness,	**10**
Close *bo*som-friend of the *maturing sun*;	**10**
Con*spiring* with him how to *load* and *bless,*	**10**
With *fruit* the vines that *round* the thatch-eves *run*;	**10**
To *bend* with *a*pples the moss'd *co*ttage-*trees*,	**10**
And fill *all* fruit with *ripe*ness to the *core*;	**10**
To *swell* the gourd, and *plump* the hazel *shells*,	**10**
With a *sweet ke*rnel; to set *bud*ding *more*,	**10**
And still *more*, later *flowers* for the *bees*,	**10**
Until they *think* warm days will never *cease*,	**10**
For *summ*er has o'er brimm'd their *clam*my *cells*.	**10**

Exercise 3: Cadence

In poetry, cadence is the rising and falling of the voice when reciting a piece. Good poetry pays attention to cadence because it influences the mood and tone of your poem. Why is this important?

It's important to understand what your expectations are and if they match the outcome of your reader's inner voice. As a page-poet, you are not present to depict the rise and falls of the poem by reading to them. They would need to define it on their own.

Below is an example of how cadence works! The arrow pointing down signifies the low pitch of your voice while reading a syllable. The arrow pointing up implies that the author expects you to read a word with a higher pitch. The dashes tell you to say the words without an intonation. Basically, a monotonous tone. Try reading these aloud.

↓ ↑ ↓ ↑ — ↓ — ↑

If you should find somebody new,

↓ ↑ ↓ ↑ — — ↑ ↑ ↓↑ — ↓

I pray that you have the courage to let me know,

↑ — — ↓ ↑ — — ↓ ↑

Let me go without looking back too,

↓ ↑ — — ↓ ↑ ↓ ↑ — — — ↓

For I won't have the strength to do so, or to go.

- 'Let Me Go' by Charissa Ong Ty

Try out these two exercises on cadence below! Let's see if you understand the use of cadence. Use different arrows to differentiate between the lower and higher pitches. Draw an arrow up when you realise that you're reading a particular word with a higher pitch and draw an arrow down for the words you read at a lower pitch.

Exercise 1: Charissa Ong - "In Loving Memory"

Like a guilty mourner he toughened his nerves,

With flowers to acknowledge the death of their love.

He knew his apology fell on deaf ears,

And on the heart that has grown numb over the years.

Exercise 2: Timothy Joshua - "Starlight"

The light in your eyes

captures all the starlight in our universe.

And so, I live within;

an insignificant speck in your eyes.

Did you read the poems with a certain pitch? Let's check your answers!

Answer 1: Charissa Ong - "In Loving Memory"

↓ — ↑ ↓ — ↑ — ↓ ↑

Like a guilty mourner he toughened his nerves,

↓ ↑ ↓ — ↑ ↓ ↑ — — ↓

With flowers to acknowledge the death of their love.

↓ ↑ ↓ ↑ — ↓ — ↑

He knew his apology fell on deaf ears,

↑ — ↓ ↑ — — ↓ ↑ — — ↓

And on the heart that has grown numb over the years.

Answer 2: Timothy Joshua - "Starlight"

↓ ↑ — ↓ ↑

The light in your eyes

↑ — ↓ ↑ — — ↓

captures all the starlight in our universe.

↓ ↑ ↓ ↑ —

And so, I live within;

↓ — ↑ — ↓ ↑ ↓

an insignificant speck in your eyes.

Getting Started

In this chapter, you will be exploring different ways to write your poems! After understanding the basics of rhyme, rhythm, meters and cadence, you're now good to go!

Feel free to play around and mix and match those methods. Break the boundaries if you have to. We will go through some exercises to build up the structure for your poems from choosing themes to dealing with the infamous writer's block.

Remember that good poetry needs to tell a compelling story, contain figurative language and tappable rhythm! You would want readers to have a pleasant, nostalgic feeling whenever they read your poems. The more emotion you evoke in a reader, the more effective it is.

Exercise 4: Exploring Your Themes

Poetry is about writing what you are passionate about in a few lines or stanzas. There are no limits as to what is the perfect theme to write poems. As the words of American poet Robert Frost, *"A poem begins as a lump in the throat, a sense of wrong, a homesickness, a lovesickness."* Adding to this quote, we'd also say, *"A poem also begins with a rumble in the belly, a feeling of joy, a pleasant feeling."*

What do you want to write about? List a few themes here. e.g. Heartbreak, friendships, comedic situations.

Theme 1:

____

Theme 2:

____

Theme 3:

____

Exercise 5: Poetic Metaphors

Figurative Language

This is arguably to be one of the most important elements in poetry. It elevates the human senses through reading and your readers are able to form mental images in their minds.

First draft example:

"My tears are falling because you made me cry."

Impact:
a. Too literal
b. Leaves no room for imagination
c. The depth of the statement seems shallow

Second draft example:

"My tears seem to be the only thing that could really quench your thirst. But, you didn't know that you were drawing water from a well that is already dry."

Impact:
a. Metaphors make the reader understand your statement from a more layered and richer perspective.

b. Beautiful story-like imagery retains in the reader's mind.

Now, it's time for you to bedazzle this unimaginative sample we have prepared for you on the next page!

Second text, first draft:

"I feel sad and lonely because you are not here with me."

Your turn:

\
____

\
____

\
____

\
____

\
____

Homophones & Homonyms

You are probably thinking, what are these two words? Are they useful in poetry? Of course! Homonyms and homophones are helpful when it comes to enhancing your vocabulary in writing.

Also, these tools come in handy in poetry especially when you want to rhyme! It helps when you are song-writing or writing raps too. There are many websites and apps online that could help you find words to rhyme.

Homophones refer to a word that has the same sound as another word but they're both spelled differently.

Example of Homophones:

ate/eight
by/buy/bye
cent/scent
dew/do/due
flower/flour

Homonyms, on the other hand are words that sound and spelled the same but mean different things.

Example of Homonyms:
1) "cool" can mean that you're chilly, in peace or in style.
2) "right" means you're correct, morally good or the direction.

Can you think of an example of homophones and homonyms? They're quite prevalent in puns. Here's one for you to roll your eyes at:

Who's righter?
Is it my wife or I?
My wife's a writer,
So that makes her righter than I!

Hm, the word 'righter' doesn't really exist does it? As a poet, you do have the 'poetic license' to invent words. Do this wisely and make sure they make sense when used in a context. William Shakespeare invented plenty of words we use today. Words from his plays like 'Unreal', 'Bandit', 'Critic' and 'Elbow' are some of his creations we still use today.

Exercise 6: Dealing with Writer's Block

Every one of us has faced writer's block. Mind-mapping is a great way to help you form ideas and thoughts creatively as you branch out from keyword to keyword until you eventually land on a creative idea you like. The brain is a mysterious organ that needs to be coaxed and woken up slowly.

Here's an example we've prepared:

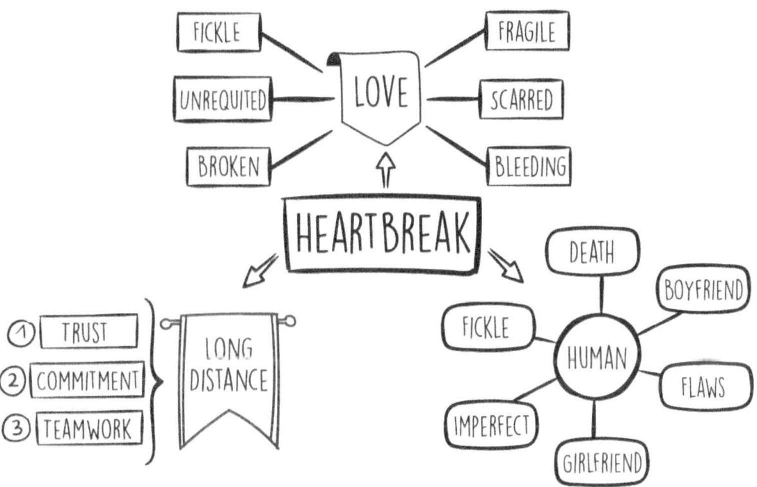

By doing this, you have already created a list of prompts for your next poem! Try it yourself. In exercise 4, you have explored some themes. Try branching them out from there.

Exercise 6: Dealing with Writer's Block

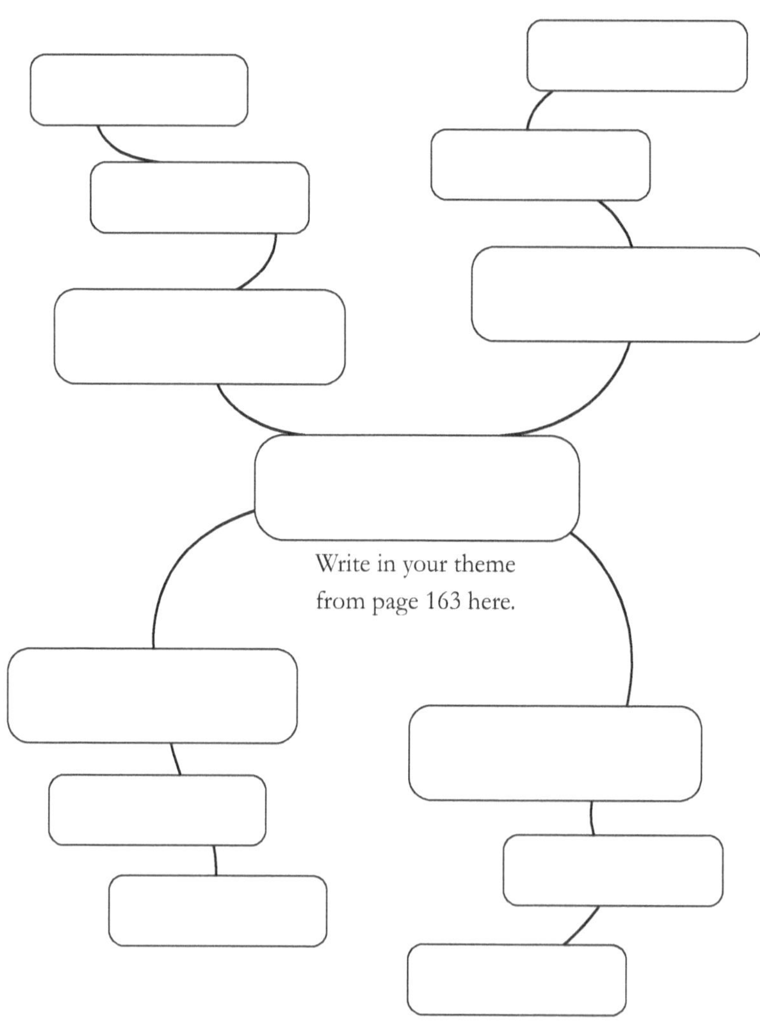

Crafting Poetry

It's time for you to hone your pen and start creating magic on paper! We have poetry prompt exercises for you to challenge your creativity and a one-poem-a-day challenge to help you practice consistency. You will only get better with constant practice. Rise to the challenge, young padawan!

Feel free to tag us on Instagram at @penwingspublishing. We would love to read and give feedback on them!

Exercise 7: Poetry Prompts

On some days, you would feel uninspired and feel like you have nothing to write about. But rest assured, this exercise will raise your poetic spirit! In this part of the practice book, you will be writing poems based on these prompts. Feel free to execute the poems in your personal renditions.

There are instances where you would end up with prose instead. Sometimes, a short paragraph conveys an idea better than a stanza ever could. Explore writing proses too.

Another tip while writing poetry, you may find that the last line of the piece usually brings the idea home. You might have a very beautiful beginning and middle, but if the ending falls flat, the whole piece might not be memorable to the reader.

Spend more time with the ending. We wouldn't want to have another 'How I Met Your Mother' or 'Game of Thrones' situation now, would we?

Turn to the next page and let your poetic spirit soar!

Exercise 7: Poetry Prompts

Prompt 1:

Write a poem based on your favorite color and the meaning your color holds.

____

____

____

____

____

____

____

____

Exercise 7: Poetry Prompts

Prompt 2:

Write about your first heartbreak.

Exercise 7: Poetry Prompts

Prompt 3:

Write about your favorite memory with the person you love.

Exercise 7: Poetry Prompts

Prompt 4:

Think of the best friendship you've ever had and explain why.

____

____

____

____

____

____

____

____

Exercise 7: Poetry Prompts

Prompt 5:

Pour out your thoughts about what patience and love mean to you.

____

____

____

____

____

____

____

____

Exercise 7: Poetry Prompts

Prompt 6:

Craft a poem about your favorite fairy tale.

Exercise 7: Poetry Prompts

Prompt 7:

Put into words about how you feel when you travel to new, unfamiliar places.

Exercise 7: Poetry Prompts

Prompt 8:

Recall one of your favorite dreams and how that dream made you feel.

____

____

____

____

____

____

____

____

____

Exercise 7: Poetry Prompts

Prompt 9:

Write a piece about body positivity.

Exercise 7: Poetry Prompts

Prompt 10:

Write a poem based on your favorite lyric.

Exercise 8: One Poem-a-Day Challenge

As always, to improve your writing, you need to constantly sharpen your writing skills! To challenge yourself, try writing one poem a day! Do not fuss over the first line but just keep writing until you reach the end of the poem. You may edit it again once you've finished your piece.

Exercise 8: One Poem-a-Day Challenge

Exercise 8: One Poem-a-Day Challenge

Exercise 8: One Poem-a-Day Challenge

Exercise 8: One Poem-a-Day Challenge

Exercise 8: One Poem-a-Day Challenge

Exercise 8: One Poem-a-Day Challenge

Exercise 8: One Poem-a-Day Challenge

Exercise 8: One Poem-A-Day Challenge

Exercise 8: One Poem-A-Day Challenge

Exercise 9: Reading Aloud, Amending & Criticism

Reading your poems aloud can help you immensely when you want to check the rhythm and meters of your pieces. When you read your poems with a clear voice, you are able to hear the flow of your desired intonation patterns. If you're not pleased with the way your poems sound, you can always make the changes in this exercise!

Another way to help you make amendments is by getting feedback from your community. Whether they are your friends, family or your readers online, it's always helpful to hear comments from people of different backgrounds. Don't be disheartened if you get criticism but receive them with an open mind! Jot down below if you have received constructive comments or ways you could improve your writing style. Critiquing yourself always works. Try putting yourself into a reader's shoes. How would you critique the work? How did it make you feel?

Constructive comments from myself and others:

____

____

____

____

____

Conclusion

Phew, what a ride! You have finally arrived at the end of the book. We hope you've enjoyed exploring different ideas and found this helpful!

We live by the quote, *"If you want to be a writer, you must do two things above all others: read a lot and write a lot,"* by the king of horror, Stephen King.

Never stop penning down your stories and thoughts on paper or typing them out on your gadgets. Read more and practice until you've got the hang of creative writing.

You've got this, I'm so proud of you!

Love,
Charissa Ong Ty
Founder of Penwings Publishing
Bestselling Author

About Penwings

Established in 2016, Penwings is a publishing house based in Malaysia and we pride ourselves with the motto,

"Let us give your pen wings."

Penwings strives to make your publishing dreams come true by giving your masterpieces a chance to be read by many. Send in your manuscripts and cover letters to: hello@penwings.com!

MIDNIGHT MONOLOGUES
By Charissa Ong Ty

No.1 Best-Selling English Poetry and Short Stories is sold in major bookstores in Malaysia, Singapore and the Philippines. #MidnightMonologues is divided into four parts: LOST, FOUND, HOPE, and Short Stories. In an age of decreased readership and short attention spans, this book aims to ignite the readers' imagination; with short, melodious writing.

QUESTIONS TO OUR ANSWERS
By Timothy Joshua

#QTOA is a poetry and fiction book containing three main chapters, centred around questions one would ask during different stages of a relationship: What are we? Where are we going? How are we getting there? The poems, juxtaposed with short stories, take readers on a deeply reflective journey as they contemplate the deepest thoughts and hopes they carry for their past and present relationships.

DAYLIGHT DIALOGUES
By Charissa Ong Ty

Back by popular demand, Charissa Ong Ty's second Poetry and Short Stories book, #DaylightDialogues, re-explores heartbreak, deep aspirations of love, self-actualization and fictional short stories.

Pushing her boundaries with more challenging technical poetry writing, she hopes her readership would appreciate Daylight Dialogues as much as they did Midnight Monologues.

MORE THAN WORDS
By Zack Shah

A diary, a love letter and a storybook all rolled into one, Zack Shah bares it all in his debut poetry collection. #MTW is a collection where each page is a small window into a world where reality and imagination are childhood friends. From the innocence of young romance to the dangers of desire, experience the entire spectrum of human emotion laced in between his crafted words.

POETHREE O' CLOCK BOXSET
By Charissa Ong Ty

Charissa Ong released a special collectible box set that includes her best-selling titles, Midnight Monologues, Daylight Dialogues along with a new illustrated poetry book, 'What Does Your Name Mean?'. The new poetry book brings readers on a journey of self-identity and addresses the failures and darkness one faces in a safe light.

MIDNIGHT MONOLOGUES AUDIOBOOK
By Charissa Ong Ty

Midnight Monologues Audiobook has two renditions. A female reader and a male reader. Sit back and relax while we read these beautiful stories out to you as you are about to go to sleep, while you're on a slow drive home from work or on a balcony with hot Camomile tea on a breezy, Saturday afternoon.

These audiobooks are available on our website as well as on international audiobook platforms.

References

Quotes

Angelou, M., 1969. I Know Why The Caged Bird Sings. 1st ed. New York: Bantam Books.

Brewer, R., 2019. 7 Toni Morrison Quotes For Writers And About Writing. [Online] Writer's Digest. Available at: <https://www.writersdigest.com/be-inspired/toni-morrison-quotes-for-writers-and-about-writing>

Crezo, A., 2014. 18 Quotes For Writers From Ernest Hemingway. [Online] Writer's Digest. Available at: <https://www.writersdigest.com/there-are-no-rules/18-quotes-for-writers-from-ernest-hemingway>

Fitzgerald, F., n.d. F. Scott Fitzgerald Quotes. [Online] Goodreads.com. Available at: <https://www.goodreads.com/author/quotes/3190.F_Scott_Fitzgerald>

Frost, R., n.d. A Quote By Robert Frost. [Online] Goodreads.com. Available at: <https://www.goodreads.com/quotes/266356-a-poem-begins-with-a-lump-in-the-throat-a>

Gaiman, N., n.d. A Quote By Neil Gaiman. [Online] Goodreads.com. Available at: <https://www.goodreads.com/author/quotes/1221698.Neil_Gaiman>

King, S., 2000. On Writing: A Memoir Of The Craft. 1st ed. New York: Scribner.

Walsh, T., 2008. Interview: Ann Aguirre, Part 1. [Online] Writer Unboxed. Available at: <https://writerunboxed.com/2008/02/22/

interview-ann-aguirre-part-1/>

Books

Albom, M., 2006. For One More Day. London: Sphere.
Austen, J., 2010. Pride and Prejudice. Surrey: Alma Classics.
Collins, S., 2011. The Hunger Games. London: Scholastic Ltd.
Hesse, H., 2017. Demian. London: Peguin Classics.
Rowling, J. K., 2014. Harry Potter and The Philosopher's Stone. London: Bloomsbury.
Sparks, N., 2004. The Notebook. 1st ed. New York: Vision.
Stedman, M. L., 2016. The Light Between Oceans. 1st ed. New York: Pocket Books.

Poems

Blake, W., n.d. The Chimney Sweeper: A Little Black Thing Among… | Poetry Foundation. [Online] Poetry Foundation. Available at: <https://www.poetryfoundation.org/poems/43653/the-chimney-sweeper-a-little-black-thing-among-the-snow>

Frost, R., n.d. Nothing Gold Can Stay By Robert Frost | Poetry Foundation. [Online] Poetry Foundation. Available at: <https://www.poetryfoundation.org/poems/148652/nothing-gold-can-stay-5c095cc5ab679>

Hughes, L., n.d. Harlem By Langston Hughes | Poetry Foundation. [Online] Poetry Foundation. Available at: <https://www.poetryfoundation.org/poems/46548/harlem>

Joshua, T., 2017. Starlight. In: Questions to Our Answers. Selangor: Penwings Publishing, p. 37.

Keats, J., n.d. "Bright Star, Would I Were Stedfast As Thou Art"… | Poetry Foundation. [Online] Poetry Foundation.

Available at: <https://www.poetryfoundation.org/poems/44468/bright-star-would-i-were-stedfast-as-thou-art>

Keats, J., n.d. To Autumn By John Keats | Poetry Foundation. [Online] Poetry Foundation. Available at: <https://www.poetryfoundation.org/poems/44484/to-autumn>

Ong, C., 2018. In Loving Memory. In: Daylight Dialogues. Selangor: Penwings Publishing , p. 20.

Shakespeare, W., 2009. Sonnet 18. In: J. Kerrigan, ed. Shakespeare's Sonnets. Victoria: Penguin Books, p. 18.

Wordsworth, W., n.d. I Wandered Lonely As A Cloud By William

Wordsworth | Poetry Foundation. [Online] Poetry Foundation. Available at: <https://www.poetryfoundation.org/poems/45521/i-wandered-lonely-as-a-cloud>

Pictures

Annie Spratt @anniespratt on Unsplash.com
Aron Visuals @aronvisuals on Unsplash.com
Kym MacKinnon @vixenly on Unsplash.com
Ricardo Resende @rresende on Unsplash.com
Sebastian Unrau @sebastion_unrau on Unsplash.com
Stepheniemeyer.com

Others

Isbn-international.org. 2014. What Is An ISBN? | International ISBN Agency. [Online] Available at: https://www.isbn-international.org/content/what-isbn

Ishiguro, K., 2014. Kazuo Ishiguro: how I wrote The
Remains of The Day in four weeks. [Online] Available
at: https://www.theguardian.com/books/2014/dec/06/
kazuo-ishiguro-the-remains-of-the-day-guardian-book-club

MasterClass, 2020. 6 Elements Of A Good Story. [Online]
MasterClass. Available at: <https://www.masterclass.com/articles/
elements-of-a-good-story#6-elements-of-a-good-story>

MasterClass, 2020. How To Develop Fictional Characters:
8 Tips For Character Development. [Online] MasterClass.
Available at: <https://www.masterclass.com/articles/
how-to-develop-fictional-characters#8-tips-for-character-development>

MasterClass, 2020. How To Write A Short Story In 5 Steps:
Writing Tips For Great Story Ideas. [Online] MasterClass.
Available at: <https://www.masterclass.com/articles/
how-to-write-a-great-short-story-writing-tips-and-exercises-for-story-ideas>

MasterClass, 2020. How To Write Poetry: 11 Rules For Poetry Writing
Beginners. [Online] MasterClass. Available at: <https://www.masterclass.
com/articles/how-to-write-poetry>

Riley, K. J., n.d. S.T.O.R.Y. Extensions!. [Online]
Available at: https://msjordanreads.com/2012/11/17/s-t-o-r-y-extensions/

Glossary

Short Story

100 Words-a-Day, pg. 52
A challenge for aspiring writers to instill consistency in writing.

Adjective, pg. 22
A word that describes a noun, giving it more information like the shape, colour, size and feelings if the noun is a person.

Book Cover, pg. 140
A book cover is any protective covering used to bind together the pages of a book.

Cover Letter, pg. 144, 145, 146
A letter of introduction attached to or accompanying another document such as a résumé or a curriculum vitae.

Flash Short Story, pg. 11
A type of short story that only consists only a few hundred words.

Flow, pg. 12, 27
A style of transitioning one sentence to another to form a seamless storyline and make it easier to read.

Genre, pg. 11, 29, 30
A style or category of art, music, or literature.

Illustrator, pg. 140
An artist who draws and designs for any medium that is needed.

Introduction, pg. 25, 46
The starting paragraph of a narrative that introduces the story.

ISBN, pg. 142,
Stands for International Standard Book Number which is a set of numbers to identify a book.

Jargon, pg. 13, 153
Words or terminologies that are obscure and rarely used which can cause confusion to readers.

Manuscript, pg. 11, 134, 135, 144
A writer's complete literary work but is yet to be published.

Moodboard, pg. 141
A visual tool that communicates visual ideas and concepts to help

Glossary

form a concrete plan.

Novel, pg. 3, 38, 145
A fictitious narrative written to entertain and typically not less than forty thousand words.

Outline, pg. 12, 44
A general description or plan showing the essential features of the short story but not the details.

Pacing, pg. 12, 24, 26
A tool that writers use to control the speed and rhythm for the events of the story.

Preposition, pg. 19, 21, 22, 23
A word that comes after a noun or pronoun to express a relation with another word.

Proofreading, pg. 14, 18, 24, 52, 93
An act of editing and highlight errors in written works.

Red Flags, pg. 12
In writing, it refers to the sensitive topics that are generally not well-received and must be crafted with taste.

Settings, pg. 34
The period and location chosen by the writer for a literary work.

Short Story, pg. 11, 14, 24, 43
A narrative with a well-developed theme and plot but notably shorter and less elaborate than a full-fledged novel.

Verb, pg. 18, 21, 23
A word that is used to describe an action, state or occurrence of a subject in a sentence.

Glossary

Poetry

Cadence, pg. 158,159
The rising and falling of the voice's intonation when reciting poetry.

Homophones, pg. 165
A word that has the same sound as another word but both are spelled differently. Like 'great' and 'grate.'

Homonyms, pg. 166
A group of words that sound or spelled the same but have different meanings. Like the word 'fly'.

Metaphors, pg. 164,
A figure of speech that makes a comparison between two subjects to produce symbolism.

Meters, pg. 151,155
A pattern of stressed and unstressed syllables found in poetry.

Mind Map, pg.167, 168
A visual diagram that helps to organize and expand rough ideas around a central topic.

Poetic License, pg. 166
A poet's liberty to depart from conventional facts, writing form or logic when writing to create a creative effect.

Prompts, pg. 170
A brief text or sentence that gives a potential idea to start writing any literary work.

Prose Poetry, pg. 170
A type of poetic verse that does not follow the formal structural or rhythmic form of traditional poetry.

Rhyme, pg. 152, 153
A literary device that highlights the repetition of identical or similar ending syllables of different words.

Rhythm, pg. 151, 155, 156
A movement that has a uniform or patterned beat of syllables to produce a good tone in poetry.

Writer's Block, pg. 167, 168
An unfortunate condition where a writer is unable to think of what to write about.